Speak the Word
Over Your Family
for Salvation

by
Harry and Cheryl Salem

Speak the Word Over Your Family for Salvation
ISBN 1-577942-85-X
Copyright © 1999 Salem Family Ministries
P.O. Box 701287
Tulsa, Oklahoma 74170

Published by Harrison House
P.O. Box 35035
Tulsa, Oklahoma 74153

Dedication

To our parents and families, through their example of household salvation and dedication, they have shown us the importance of family, salvation and relationship with God. Through good times and bad they've remained steadfast in their commitment and strength, which comes from God.

List the names of the people you'll be praying for on this page.

Introduction

A few years ago the Lord spoke to our hearts and challenged us to begin to pray His Word out loud each day. I thought I was already doing that, but I quickly learned that I was only partially doing what He wanted me to do. God told us to activate His Word by praying it over our loved ones and friends each day.

The Lord said to me, "You think you have been praying My Word, but you have only been reading and saying My Word to me! I want you to write My Word out so that you can insert every-one's name into My Word, then I want you to go down the list of all the people you are to pray for each day and indi-vidually pray, not just say the words but pray, with each person's name inserted right into My Word! Pray every word,

My Word, out loud to Me. I will watch over it and perform it concerning the people whose names are inserted into each prayer. You just activate My Word by praying it into the atmosphere."

We immediately began to dig through the Word, write out the scriptures and allow the Holy Spirit to show us how to pray more effectively. After we wrote out just a few prayers, the Lord spoke to us again. This time He said, "Now that you know how to pray My Word, I want you to search my Word for effective scriptures to pray each day."

As we searched the Word we began to realize the vital importance of speaking God's Words and not our own. Jeremiah 1:12 says, "Then said the Lord to me, You have seen well, for I am alert and active, watching over my Word to perform it."

Through this scripture we began to realize that God's Word activates the angels to accomplish God's will in our lives on this earth! That's why God *spoke* the world into existence, as an example to us, His children, of how to be creative and have God's kind of creative power and force upon this earth.

In Isaiah 44:26, "[The Lord] who confirms the word of His servant and performs the counsel of His messengers..." we quickly saw that God listens to what we say and then, because He set up the "power of the creative tongue" in Genesis chapter one, He performs through His messengers our words. That's why our words need to be His Words!

Isaiah 55:11 went on to further establish the importance of our speaking and our praying when it said, "So shall My Word be that goes forth out of My mouth: it shall not return to Me void [without producing any effect, useless], but it shall accomplish that which I please and purpose, and it shall prosper in the thing for which I sent it."

We believe the most powerful scripture on speaking the Word of God out of our mouths when we pray is Psalm 107:20, "He sends forth His Word and heals them and rescues them from the pit and destruction." You might say, "Well, of course, when God sends His Word it works, but it's me doing the sending." NO!!!! You aren't doing the sending. You don't have any power to make words travel through time and space and get on a person's life. But God not only has this power, He uses us to speak His Word out of our mouths and then through the supernatural ways of God these words transcend all realms: the natural realm, the emotional and mental (soulish) realm, and the supernatural realm. These three realms are all reality! God's Word moves into all realms the minute it comes out of our mouths and begins to "self-fulfill."

Isaiah 61:11 says, "For as [surely as] the earth brings forth its shoots, and as a garden causes what is sown in it to spring forth, so [surely] the Lord God will cause rightness and justice and praise to spring forth before all the nations [through the self-fulfilling power of His Word]."

What a powerful scripture! God's Word has a built in self-fulfilling power! It must do what it says it will do! When we say it out of our mouths concerning us or anyone else the Word must self-fulfill! Get the revelation of this powerful action when you pray and know that the minute you say it out of your mouth it is a done deal! It's done!

You might be thinking, "But what about a person's free will to choose for themselves?" That's a very good question and we have heard it many times since the Lord had us start to teach this way of praying. We asked the Lord about it.

You know the Father God always has the answer to all of our questions even before we ask them! The Lord began to direct us to some of the scriptures that you are about to learn to pray over your family and loved ones.

Acts 26:18 is one of the first ones that God showed us to pray over our lost loved ones. It says, "To open their eyes that they may turn from darkness to light and from the power of Satan to God, so that they may thus receive forgiveness and release from their sins and a place and portion among those who are consecrated and purified by faith in Me."

As we began to pray our loved ones' names into this scripture we soon realized the key here is that we are CALLING them. When you call someone on the telephone they answer! When you call your dog he comes. When you call your children to come in for dinner they come!

There is a great spiritual power in CALLING them! Then notice we are calling them OUT OF DARKNESS INTO THE LIGHT! It's very important to notice that those loved ones have been making decisions in the past based upon being in the dark. When you call them out of darkness into the light of God and then they make a decision, it is not based upon the darkness they have been living in their minds. You have called them out of darkness into God's light and now they can make decisions based upon the light that they came into WHEN YOU CALLED THEM!

Let's look at another scripture we have been praying that will help prove this issue. Look at 1 Peter 2:9, "But you are a chosen race, a royal priesthood, a dedicated nation, [God's] own purchased, special people, that you may set forth the wonderful deeds and display the virtues and perfections of Him Who called you out of darkness into His marvelous light."

Once again there is the "calling out of darkness" action. By inserting the person's name that you are praying for, you are literally calling them by name out of darkness and giving them the opportunity to come into the light and make decisions for their future based upon the light and not the darkness!

As you go on through the scriptures that are outlined in the next few pages remember to speak them out loud. I recommend you do it morning and night. Don't ever do it while the ones you are praying for are listening. It's not them hearing you that makes a difference. It's you being obedient to speak God's Word out of your mouth concerning them and then God performing what you have spoken!

Morning and night is significant because the Bible says in Revelation 12:10, "...for the accuser of our brethren, he who keeps bringing before our God charges against them day and night..." If Satan stands and accuses day and night then I feel it is important to speak "God's Word as we pray day and night to counteract the accuser's words!

We were ministering in a church when this revelation of how to pray for your loved ones was fresh in our thinking. We were just beginning to grasp the full weight of what God was calling us to do and to teach. We shared the concept in one of the services and challenged the people to stop JUST praying, "Oh, God, save so and so and such and such..." which had gotten no results. We challenged them to write out the names of their loved ones, family members, friends, and co-workers that they had been praying for and begin to speak the Word over them day and night.

When we returned to this same church eight months later, a woman who had been in our previous meeting came up to us with a big smile on her face and a wonderful testimony to share with us. She began to tell us how, in the meeting eight months prior, she had written several names in her Bible of close loved ones that she had prayed for but had seen no results. She opened her Bible and showed how in only eight months she had already crossed off four of the names!

She said, "I did just what you said. I quit begging God, and worrying God, and I started speaking God's Word over them." Within only a few weeks, her brother and sister-in-law whom she had been praying for and witnessing to for years with no positive response, called her and asked how to get to her church.

She told them that she would come by and pick them up. They came to church and because they were in the light and not in the darkness when the altar call was given, they both gave their lives to Jesus! Hallelujah! Did she supercede their will by speaking the Word of God over them? No, but she did give them an opportunity to make choices for their lives and their futures based upon being in the light instead of making decisions while still in darkness!

She went on to tell how her father who lived in another state would not respond to her witnessing so she simply spoke the Word of God over him and believed God to "watch over His Word to perform it." Not much time passed and her father who was a widower met a lady and really liked her. This lady was saved and went to church so to be with her he went to church. They began to get close, and to make a beautiful love story short, he got saved and completely gave his life to Jesus!

What's so interesting to us about

this story is that the daughter had absolutely nothing in the natural to do with her father finding Jesus. She did not have to take him to church. She did not do anything, EXCEPT speak the Word of God over her daddy and sit back and watch God fulfill His Word!

The stories of receiving Jesus are always TO BE CONTINUED... because with God, LIFE is the key word and life goes on and on!

As we began to share this more and more with people Harry had what I call a "mini-vision." He said the Holy Ghost impressed this upon his heart. Whatever you want to call it, Harry got the point. The Holy Spirit showed Harry how one day he would be in Heaven and God would say to him, "Well done, My son." Then, as he went on into Heaven he would meet his earthly dad who went home to be with

Jesus in 1968.

He said his earthly daddy started telling him how proud he was of him for getting all these people saved and healed and filled with the Holy Ghost. His dad was so proud of how his son had a godly marriage, family, and how his grandchildren loved Jesus so much. Harry said about this time in the impression (vision) he was feeling pretty good about himself. Then his earthly daddy would turn to him and say, "But where is my brother? Where is my sister? Where is my family? You knew them by name, you knew where they lived, you knew their addresses and their phone numbers. Why didn't you get them to Heaven?"

Harry and I began to understand that this is our opportunity to lay aside any differences that we might have with any and all family members and begin to speak God's Word over them. All of a sudden earthly values didn't seem to hold any value. All that really matters is that all of our loved ones have an opportunity to receive the greatest gift of all...JESUS!

We began to speak the Word of God over any and all of his family and mine, too, that we weren't sure of their relationship with Jesus. Even if we were speaking the Word over some who already knew Jesus, that would be all right because every one will benefit from the Word of God getting on them!

Several months passed before we had an opportunity to go to some of these loved ones and spend time with them, but God made a way. For many of them it had been thirty years since there had been any contact. But God doesn't forget anyone. He wants everyone saved, healed, and filled with His Spirit.

We led many of them to Jesus when we saw them. We planted many seeds of love and acceptance into the others. EVERYTHING IS A SEED and it all produces a harvest. Above all, there was restoration of a thirty year separation. The beauty of it all is that those precious loved ones planted wonderful seeds back into our lives! That was an immediate harvest! We are not the Saviour, we just do our part and speak the Word of God and be available if God chooses to use us to do anything else!

We encourage you to stay strong. Don't let Satan get you discouraged. That really means you have taken your eyes off of your Saviour and have put your eyes back on the problem and circumstance. Remember, Romans 4:17 says, "Calling those things that be not as though they were..." Don't call your loved ones or talk about them as if they will always be the way they are now.

NO!!! Talk about them as if they are already walking in the full light of God. Talk to them as if they are, treat them as if they are! You will be amazed at what God will do when you honor His Word. The word "honor" in the Hebrew language means "to open the door." So open the door of God's Word into all your loved ones' lives by speaking God's Word over their lives. The Word works when your work the Word!

When Jesus called Simon, Peter, Simon was anything but God's rock! But Jesus was "calling those things that be not as though they were." If it's good enough for Jesus to practice "calling", I believe we ought to do it, too, and get "Jesus" kind of results!

On the next pages you will find many scriptures already written out so you can just insert your loved ones' names and speak it out of your mouth morning and night. Do it, and watch God do His thing!

Remember to pray in your prayer language after you have spoken God's Word and then listen to what the Spirit of God has to say back to you. We have left room for you to write down many of the revelations that God will give you. This is exciting! You are about to change your life and many other lives, too! Go for it!

The Word works when you work the Word!

I pray that the God of our Lord Jesus Christ, the Father of glory, may grant _____ a spirit of wisdom and revelation [of insight into mysteries and secrets] in the [deep and intimate] knowledge of Him. By having the eyes of _____'s heart flooded with light, so that _____ can know and understand the hope to which He has called _____, and how rich is His glorious inheritance in the saints (His set-apart ones). And [so that _____ can know and understand] what is the immeasurable and unlimited and surpassing greatness of His power in and for _____, who believe(s), as demonstrated in the working of His mighty strength, which He exerted in Christ when He raised Him from the dead and seated Him at

Day One
Ephesians 1:17-23

His [own] right hand in the heavenly [places], far above all rule and authority and power and dominion and every name that is named [above every title that can be conferred], not only in this age and in this world, but also in the age and the world which are to come. And He has put all things under His feet and has appointed Him the universal and supreme Head of the church [a headship exercised throughout the church], which is His body, the fullness of Him Who fills all in all [for in that body lives the full measure of Him Who makes everything complete, and Who fills everything everywhere with Himself].

I encourage you to pray one name at a time all the way through the scripture out loud.

After you have finished praying all the names on your prayer list then I invite you to pray in your prayer language or just fellowship with God. Many times you will receive the interpretation of your prayers when you listen and be quiet. This is a great way to meditate on God's Word. Learn to listen, too! (Please use the space provided to write down any thoughts you might want to remember).

_____

_____

_____

_____

_____

_____

_____

_____

_____

_____

_____

Day Two
Ephesians 3:14-21

For this reason [seeing the greatness of this plan by which _____ is built together in Christ], _____ bows his/her knees before the Father of our Lord Jesus Christ, for whom every family on earth and in heaven is named [that Father from Whom all fatherhood takes its title and derives its name].

May He grant _____ out of the rich treasury of His glory to be strengthened and reinforced with mighty power in the inner man by the [Holy] Spirit [Himself indwelling _____'s innermost being and personality]. May Christ through _____'s faith [actually] dwell (settle down, abide, make His permanent home) in _____'s heart! May _____ be rooted deep in love and founded securely on love,

that _____ may have the power
and be strong to apprehend and grasp
with all the saints [God's devoted people, the experience of that love] what is
the breadth and length and height and
depth [of it]; [That _____ may
really come] to know [practically,
through experience for himself/herself]
the love of Christ, which far surpasses
mere knowledge [without experience];
that _____ may be filled [through
all his/her being], unto all the fullness
of God [may have the richest measure
of the divine Presence, and become a
body wholly filled and flooded with
God Himself!]

Now to Him Who, by (in conse-
quence of) the [action of His] power
that is at work within _____ is
able to [carry out His purpose and] do
superabundantly, far over and above all
that _____ dares ask or think
[infinitely beyond _____'s highest

prayers, desires, thoughts, hopes, or dreams].

To Him be glory in the church and in Christ Jesus throughout all generations forever and ever.
Amen (so be it).

For your prayer thoughts. Remember to meditate (be quiet and listen to God) and pray in your prayer language.

And _____
will know the truth
and the truth will set
_____ free.

Day Three
John 8:32

Luke 10:19

Jesus has given _____
authority and power to trample upon
serpents and scorpions, and [physical
and mental strength and ability] over
all the power that the enemy (possess-
es) and nothing shall in any way harm

_____.

John 3:16

For God so greatly loved and dearly
prized the world that He [even] gave up
His only begotten (unique) Son, so that
_____, who believes in (trusts in,
clings to, relies on) Him shall not perish
(come to destruction, or be lost) but
_____ has eternal (everlasting) life.

Remember to pray and meditate.

A place for your prayer thoughts.

_____
_____
_____
_____
_____
_____
_____
_____
_____
_____
_____
_____
_____
_____
_____
_____
_____
_____
_____
_____

_____ will
make a joyful noise to
the Lord, yes, even all
our lands! _____
will serve the Lord
with gladness! _____
will come before His
presence with singing!

Day Four
Psalm 100

_____ will know (perceive,
recognize, and understand with
approval) that the Lord is God! It is He
who has made _____ and not we
ourselves (and _____ is (am)
His!).

_____ is (am) His people and
the sheep of His pasture.

_____ will enter into His gates
with thanksgiving and a thank offering
and into His courts with praise!
_____ will be thankful and
say so to Him, _____ will bless
and affectionately praise His name!

31

For the Lord is good; His mercy and loving-kindness are everlasting, His faithfulness and truth endure to all generations.

Prayer changes things!

A place for your prayer thoughts.

_____

_____

_____

_____

_____

_____

_____

_____

_____

_____

_____

_____

_____

_____

I thank you Lord that you open _____'s eyes that _____ may turn from darkness to light and from the power of Satan to God, so that _____ may receive forgiveness and release from his/her sins and a place and portion among those who are consecrated and purified by faith in Christ.

Day Five
Acts 26:18

"If my people...will humble themselves and pray...I will hear their cry and I will answer them," says God to you!

Pray and listen to God!

_____

_____

_____

_____

_____

_____

Day Six
2 Corinthians
5:20, 21

I thank you, Lord, that _____ is Christ's ambassador, God making His appeal as it were through _____.

_____ [as Christ's personal representative] begs you for Christ's sake to lay hold of the divine favor [now offered to everyone] and thank You, Lord, that _____ is reconciled to God. For _____ 's sake God made Christ [virtually] to be sin Who knew no sin, so that in and through Him _____ might become [endued with, viewed as being in, and example of] the righteousness of God [what _____ ought to be, approved and acceptable and in right relationship with Christ, by Christ's goodness].

The Word works!

_____

_____

I thank You, Lord, that grace and spiritual blessing be to _____ and [soul] peace from God the Father and our Lord Jesus Christ

Day Seven
Galatians 1:3-5

(the Messiah) be _____'s. I thank You, Lord, that Christ gave (yielded) Himself up [to atone] for _____'s sins [and to save and sanctify _____], in order to rescue and deliver _____ from this present wicked age and world order, in accordance with the will and purpose and plan of our God and Father. To Christ [be ascribed all] the glory through all the ages of the ages and the eternities of the eternities!

Amen (so be it).

_____

_____

_____

Day Eight
Galatians 3:13,14

Christ purchased
_____'s
freedom [redeeming
_____] from
the curse (doom) of
the Law [and its con-
demnation] by [Him-
self] becoming a curse for _____,
for it is written [in the Scriptures],
Cursed is everyone who hangs on a tree
(is crucified); To the end that through
[_____ 's receiving] Christ Jesus,
the blessing [promised] to Abraham
might come upon _____, so that
_____ through faith might receive
[the realization of] the promise of the
[Holy] Spirit.

Write down what God says to you!

_____

_____

_____

_____

_____

_____ will
bless (affectionately,
gratefully praise) the
Lord, O _____'s
soul; and all that
is (deepest) within

Day Nine
Psalm 103:1-6

_____, _____
will bless His holy
name! _____ will bless (affectionately, gratefully praise) the Lord, O
_____'s soul, and _____
will not forget (one of) all His benefits
Who forgives (every one of) all
_____'s iniquities, Who heals
(each one of) all_____'s diseases,
Who redeems _____'s life from
the pit and corruption, Who beautifies,
dignifies, and crowns _____ with
loving-kindness and tender mercy;
Who satisfies _____'s mouth
(_____'s necessity and desire at
his/her personal age and situation)
with good so that _____'s youth,
renewed, is like the eagle's [strong,

37

overcoming, and soaring]! The Lord executes righteousness and justice (not for _____ only, but) for all who are oppressed.

Prayer Thoughts...

_____

_____

_____

_____

_____

_____

_____

_____

_____

_____

_____

_____

_____

_____

_____

_____

_____ who dwell(s) in the secret place of the Most High shall remain stable and fixed under the shadow of the Almighty [Whose power no foe can withstand]. _____ will say of the Lord, "You are my Refuge and my Fortress, my God; on You I lean and rely, and in You I [confidently] trust!" For [then] the Lord will deliver _____ from the snare of the fowler and from the deadly pestilence. [Then] He will cover _____ with His pinions, and under His wings shall _____ trust and find refuge; His truth and His faithfulness are a shield and a buckler. _____ shall not be afraid of the terror of the night, nor of the arrow (the evil plots and slanders of the wicked) that flies by day, nor of the pestilence that stalks in darkness, nor of

Day Ten
Psalm 91

the destruction and sudden death that surprise and lay waste at noonday. A thousand may fall at _____ 's side, and ten thousand at his/her right hand, but it shall not come near him/her. Only a spectator shall _____ be, [himself/herself inaccessible in the secret place of the Most High] as _____ witness(es) the reward of the wicked. Because _____ has (have) made the Lord his/her refuge, and the Most High his/her dwelling place, there shall no evil befall _____, nor any plague or calamity come near _____'s tent.

Pray in the Spirit! God will talk to you.

_____

_____

_____

_____

_____

_____

_____

Day Eleven
Psalm 91:11-16

For He will give His angels [especial] charge over _____ to accompany and defend and preserve _____ in all his/her ways [of obedience and service]. They shall bear _____ up on their hands, lest _____ dash(es) his/her foot against a stone. _____ shall tread upon the lion and adder: the young lion and the serpent shall _____ trample underfoot. Because _____ has (have) set his/her love upon the Lord, therefore the Lord will deliver _____; The Lord will set _____ on high, because he/she knows and understands the Lord's Name [has a personal knowledge of the Lord's mercy, love, and kindness-trusts and relies on the Lord, knowing that the Lord will never forsake

_____, no, never]. _____
shall call upon the Lord, and the Lord
will answer him/her; The Lord will be
with _____ in trouble, The Lord
will deliver _____ and honor
him/her. With long life the Lord will
satisfy _____ and show him/her
the Lord's salvation.

*The Word works when you work the
Word!*

_____

_____

_____

_____

_____

_____

_____

_____

_____

_____

_____

I thank You, Lord, that _____ has (have) faith (a firm relying trust) and does (do) not doubt. I thank You, Father God, that You will not only do

Day Twelve
Matthew 21:21-22

what has been done to the fig tree when it was cursed and it withered and died, but even if _____ say(s) to this mountain, "Be taken up and cast into the sea, it will be done." And whatever _____ ask(s) for in prayer, having faith and [really] believing, _____ will receive, in Jesus name. Amen (so be it.)

_____

_____

_____

_____

_____

_____

_____

Day Thirteen

Matthew 22:37-39

_____ will love the Lord his/her God with all his/her heart and with all his/her soul and with all his/her mind (intellect). This is the great (most important, principal) and first commandment. And the second is like it: _____ will love his/her neighbor as he/she does himself/herself in Jesus' name. Amen (so be it.)

_____

_____

_____

_____

_____

_____

_____

_____

_____

The Spirit of the Lord is upon

_____,

because The Father God has anointed

_____ to

preach the good news (the Gospel) to the poor; He has sent _____ to announce release to the captives and recovery of sight to the blind, to send forth as delivered those who are oppressed [who are downtrodden, bruised, crushed, and broken down by calamity], to proclaim the accepted and acceptable year of the Lord [the day when salvation and the free favors of God profusely abound.]

Day Fourteen
Luke 4:18-19

_____

_____

_____

_____

_____

Day Fifteen
Mark 16:15-18

And Jesus said to _____, "Go into all the world and preach and publish openly the good news (the Gospel) to every creature [of the whole human race]. _____ who believes (who adheres to and trusts in and relies on the Gospel and Jesus Who it sets forth] and is baptized will be saved (from the penalty of eternal death); But he who does not believe [who does not adhere to and trust in and rely on the Gospel and Jesus Whom it sets forth] will be condemned. And these attesting signs will accompany _____ who believes: in Jesus' name _____ will drive out demons; _____ will speak in new languages; _____ will pick up serpents; and [even] if _____ drinks anything deadly, it will not hurt _____; _____ will lay his/her hands on the sick, and the sick will get well, in Jesus' mighty and miraculous name. Amen, (so be it.)

_____

_____

_____

_____

_____

_____

_____

_____

_____

_____

_____

_____

_____

_____

_____

_____

_____

_____

Day Sixteen
Jeremiah 29: 11-14

(This is a word from the Lord to the person(s) you are praying for today).

For I know the thoughts and plans that I have for _____, says the Lord, thoughts and plans for welfare and peace and not for evil, to give _____ hope in his/her final outcome. Then _____ will call upon Me, and _____ will come and pray to Me, and I, the Lord, will hear and heed _____. Then _____ will seek Me, inquire for, and require Me (as a vital necessity) and find Me, the Lord, when _____ searches for Me with all his/her heart. I will be found by _____, says the Lord, and I will release _____ from captivity and gather _____ from all the nations and all the places to which I have driven _____, says

the Lord, and I will bring _____
back to the place from which I caused
_____ to be carried away captive.

_____

_____

_____

_____

_____

_____

_____

_____

_____

_____

_____

_____

_____

_____

_____

_____

_____

_____

Day Seventeen
Isaiah 43:18-19

_____ will not (earnestly) remember the former things; neither consider the things of old. Behold, the Lord is doing a new thing for _____! Now it springs forth: _____ will perceive it and know it and will give heed to it! God will even make a way in the wilderness and rivers in the desert for _____, in Jesus name. Amen, (so be it).

Isaiah 44:3

For the Lord will pour water upon _____ who is thirsty, and floods upon the dry ground. The Lord will pour His Spirit upon _____'s offspring, and The Lord's blessing upon _____'s descendants. And they shall spring up among the grass like willows or poplars by the watercourses, in Jesus' name. Amen, (so be it).

The Lord has put His Words in _____'s mouth and has covered _____ with the shadow of His hand.

Day Eighteen
Isaiah 51:16

Philippians 1:9-11

And this I pray: that _____'s love may abound yet more and more and extend to its fullest development in knowledge and all keen insight [that _____'s love may display itself in greater depth of acquaintance and more comprehensive discernment], so that _____ may surely learn to sense what is vital, and approve and prize what is excellent and of real value [recognizing the highest and the best, and distinguishing the moral differences], and that _____ may be untainted and pure and unerring and blameless [so that with a heart sincere and certain and unsullied, _____ may approach] the day of Christ [not stumbling nor causing others to stumble]. May _____ abound in and be filled with the fruits of righteousness (of right standing with God and right doing) which come through Jesus Christ (the Anointed One), to the honor and praise of God [that His glory may be both manifested and recognized].

_____

_____

_____

_____

_____

_____

_____

_____

_____

_____

_____

_____

Day Ninteen
1 Peter 2:9-12

_____ is a chosen race, a royal priesthood, a dedicated nation, [God's] own purchased special person, that _____ may set forth the wonderful deeds and display the virtues and perfections of Him Who called _____ out of darkness into His marvelous light. Once _____ was not a people at all, but now _____ is God's person; once _____ was unpitied, but now _____ is pitied and has received mercy. _____ will abstain from the sensual urges (the evil desires, the passions of the flesh, his/her lower nature) that wage war against his/her soul. _____ will conduct himself/herself properly (honorably, righteously) among his/her peers, so that, although they may slander _____

as an evildoer, [yet] they may be witnessing _____'s good deeds
[come to] glorify God in the day of
inspection [when God shall look upon
_____ as a pastor or shepherd
looks over his flock] in Jesus' name.
Amen, (so be it.)

_____

_____

_____

_____

_____

_____

_____

_____

_____

_____

_____

_____

_____

_____

For the eyes of the Lord are upon _____ (who is upright and in right standing with God), and His ears are attentive to _____'s prayer. But the face of the Lord is against those who practice evil [to oppose _____, to frustrate, and defeat _____] in Jesus' name. Amen, (so be it).

Day Twenty
1 Peter 3:12

Philippians 4:13

_____ has strength for all things in Christ Who empowers him/her. [_____ is ready for anything and equal to anything through Him Who infuses inner strength into _____; _____ is self-sufficient in Christ's sufficiency].

Proverbs 18:16

_____'s gift makes room for him/her and brings him/her before great men.

Day Twenty one
Philippians 4:6-
9,11

_____ will not fret or have any anxiety about anything, but in every circumstance and in everything, by prayer and petition (definite requests), with thanksgiving, _____ will make his/her wants known to God. And God's peace [shall be _____'s, that tranquil state of a soul assured of its salvation through Christ, and so fearing nothing from God and being content with its earthly lot of whatever sort that is, that peace] which transcends all understanding shall garrison and mount guard over _____'s heart and mind in Christ Jesus. Whatever is true, whatever is worthy of reverence and is honorable and seemly, whatever is just, whatever is pure, whatever is lovely and lovable, whatever is kind and winsome and gracious, if there is any virtue and excellence, if there is anything worthy of praise, _____ will think on and weigh and take account of these things [fix his/her mind on them].

_____ will practice what he/she has learned and received and heard and seen and _____ will model his/her way of living on it, and the God of peace (of untroubled, undisturbed well-being) will be with _____.

_____ has learned how to be content (satisfied to the point where he/she is not disturbed or disquieted) in whatever state that he/she is in, in the mighty name of Jesus. Amen, (so be it).

Prayer Journal

_____

_____

_____

_____

_____

_____

Day Twenty-two
Colossians 1:9-14

For this reason we also from the day we heard of it, have not ceased to pray and make [special] request for _____, [asking] that _____ may be filled with the full (deep and clear) knowledge of Christ's will in all spiritual wisdom [in comprehensive insight into the ways and purposes of God] and in understanding and discernment of spiritual things—that _____ may walk (live and conduct himself/herself) in a manner worthy of the Lord, fully pleasing to Him and desiring to please Him in all things, bearing fruit in every good work and steadily growing and increasing in and by the knowledge of God [with fuller, deeper, and clearer insight, acquaintance, and recognition]. [We pray] that _____ may be invigorated and strengthened with all power according to the might of Christ's glory, [to exercise] every kind of endurance and patience (perseverance and forbearance) with joy, giving thanks to the Father, Who has qualified and made _____ fit to share the portion which is the inheritance of the saints (God's holy people) in the Light. [The Father] has delivered and drawn _____ to Himself out of the control and the dominion of darkness and has transferred _____ into the Kingdom of the Son of His love, in whom we have our redemption through Christ's blood, [which means] the forgiveness of _____'s sins.

Pray in the Spirit!

_____

_____

_____

_____

_____

Day Twenty-
three

Proverbs 16:3

_____
rolls his/her works
upon the Lord
[_____ com-
mits and trusts them
wholly to Him; He
will cause _____'s
thoughts to become
agreeable to His will, and] so shall
_____'s plans be established and
succeed in Jesus' name. Amen, (so be it).

Proverbs 15:30

The light in the eyes [of _____
whose heart is joyful] rejoices the hearts
of others, and good news nourishes
_____'s bones in Jesus' name.
Amen, (so be it).

Write down your thoughts.

_____

_____

_____

_____

_____

_____ has a glad heart and because he/she has a glad heart _____ has a continual feast (regardless of circumstances).

Proverbs 15:4

_____ has a gentle tongue which brings with it healing power and is a tree of life to those who hear it in Jesus' name. Amen, (so be it).

Remember: the Word works!

_____
_____
_____
_____
_____
_____
_____
_____
_____
_____

Day Twenty-five

Psalm 1:1-3

Blessed (happy, fortunate, prosperous, and enviable) is _____ who walks and lives not in the counsel of the ungodly [following their advice, their plans and purposes], nor does _____ stand [submissive and inactive] in the path where sinners walk, nor does _____ sit down [to relax and rest] where the scornful [and the mockers] gather. But _____'s delight and desire is in the law of the Lord, and on His law [the precepts, the instructions, the teachings of God] does _____ habitually meditate (ponder and study) by day and by night. And _____ shall be like a tree firmly planted [and tended] by the streams of water, ready to bring forth its fruit in its season; its leaf also shall not fade or wither; and everything _____ does shall prosper [and come to maturity].

Let all _____'s enemies be ashamed and sorely troubled; let them turn back and be put to shame suddenly.

Isaiah 1:19

Day Twenty-six
Psalm 6:10

_____ is willing and obedient and he/she shall eat the good of the land in Jesus' name. Amen, (so be it).

_____

_____

_____

_____

_____

_____

_____

_____

_____

_____

_____

_____

_____

Day Twenty-seven

Isaiah 54:17

But no weapon that is formed against _____ shall prosper, and every tongue that shall rise against _____ in judgment he/she shall show to be in the wrong. This [peace, righteousness, security, triumph over opposition] is the heritage of _____, the servant of the Lord [in whom the ideal Servant of the Lord is reproduced]; this is the righteousness or the vindication which he/she obtains from the Lord [this is that which the Lord imparts to _____ as his/her justification], in Jesus' name. Amen, (so be it).

Write down your thoughts.

_____

_____

_____

Day Twenty-eight
Isaiah 55:2B-3,6

_____ will hearken diligently to the Lord, and _____ will eat what is good, and he/she will let his/her soul delight itself in fatness [the profuseness of spiritual joy]. _____ will incline his/her ear [submitting and consenting to the divine will] and _____ will come to the Lord; he/she will hear, and his/her soul will revive; and the Lord will make an everlasting covenant or league with _____, even the sure mercy (kindness, goodwill, and compassion) promised to David will be his/hers. _____ will seek, inquire for, and require the Lord while He may be found [claiming the Lord by necessity and by right]; _____ will call upon the Lord while He is near.

Day Twenty-
nine
Isaiah 55:8-13

The Lord says,
"_____, My
thoughts are not
your thoughts nei-
ther are your ways
My ways. For as the
heavens are higher
than the earth, so are
My ways higher than your ways and My
thoughts higher than your thoughts.
For as the rain and snow come down
from the heavens, and return not there
again, but water the earth and make it
bring forth and sprout, that it may give
seed to the sower and bread to the eater,
so shall My Word be that goes forth out
of My mouth: it shall not return to Me
void (without producing any effect,
useless), but it shall accomplish that
which I please and purpose, and it shall
prosper in the thing for which I sent it.
For you, _____, shall go out
[from the spiritual exile caused by sin
and evil into the holyland] with joy and

be led forth [by your Leaders, the Lord Himself, and His Word] with peace; the mountains and the hills shall break forth before you, _____, into singing, and all the trees of the field shall clap their hands. Instead of the thorn shall come up the cypress tree, and instead of the brier shall come up the myrtle tree; and it shall be to the Lord for a name of renown, for an ever-lasting sign [of jubilant exaltation] and memorial [to His praise], which shall not be cut off to you, _____, in the name of Jesus. Amen, (so be it)."

_____

_____

_____

_____

_____

_____

_____

_____

_____

Day Thirty
Isaiah 59:21

This is a word from the Lord to you, _____. _____, As for Me, this is My covenant or league with you: My Spirit, Who is upon you, [and Who writes the law of God inwardly on the heart], and My words which I have put in your mouth, _____, shall not depart out of your mouth, or out of the mouths of your [true, spiritual] children, or out to the mouths of your children's children, says the Lord, to you, _____, from henceforth and forever in Jesus' name. Amen, (so be it).

The Lord is good to _____, and His tender mercies are over all His works [the entirety of things created].	Day Thirty-one Psalm 145:9

Proverbs 12:1a-2a

_____ loves instruction, correction and loves knowledge. _____ is a good man /woman and _____ obtains favor from the Lord.

Pray and expect a miracle for your family!

_____
_____
_____
_____
_____
_____
_____
_____
_____
_____

Day Thirty-two

Isaiah 60:1-5

_____ shall arise [from the depression and the prostration in which circumstances have kept him/her. _____ shall rise to a new life]! _____ shall shine [be radiant with the glory of the Lord], for _____'s light has come, and the glory of the Lord has risen upon _____. For behold, darkness shall cover the earth, and dense darkness [all] peoples, but the Lord shall arise upon _____, and His glory shall be seen on _____, and nations shall come to _____'s light, and kings to the brightness of _____'s rising. _____ will lift up his/her eyes round about him/her and see! They all gather themselves together, they come to _____. _____'s sons shall come from afar, and his/her daughters shall be carried and nursed in the arms. Then _____ shall see and be radiant, and his/her heart shall thrill and tremble with joy [at the glorious deliverance] and be enlarged; because the abundant wealth of the [Dead] Sea shall be turned to _____, unto _____ shall the nations come with their treasures in Jesus' name. Amen (so be it).

Don't forget to pray in the Spirit!

_____
_____
_____
_____
_____
_____
_____
_____
_____
_____
_____

Day Thirty-three

Isaiah 61:1-3, 10, 11

The Spirit of the Lord God is upon _____, because the Lord has anointed and qualified _____ to preach the Gospel of good tidings to the meek, the poor, and afflicted; He has sent _____ to bind up and heal the brokenhearted, to proclaim liberty to the [physical and spiritual] captives and the opening of the prison and of the eyes to those who are bound, to proclaim the acceptable year of the Lord [the year of His favor] and the day of vengeance of our God, to comfort all who mourn, to grant [consolation and joy] to those who mourn in Zion—to give them an ornament (a garland or diadem) of beauty instead of ashes, the oil of joy instead of mourning, the garment [expressive] of praise instead of a heavy, burdened, and failing spirit—

that they may be called oaks of righteousness [lofty, strong, and magnifi-
cent, distinguished for uprightness, justice, and right standing with God], the
planting of the Lord, that He may be
glorified. _____ will greatly
rejoice in the Lord, his/her soul will
exult in our God; for He has clothed
_____ with the garments of
salvation, He has covered _____
with the robes of righteousness, as a
bridegroom decks himself with a garland, and as a bride adorns herself with
her jewels. For as [surely as] the earth
brings forth its shoots, and as a garden
causes what is sown in it to bring forth,
so [surely] the Lord God will cause
rightness and justice and praise to
spring forth before all the nations
[through the self-fulfilling power of His
word] in _____'s life in Jesus'
name. Amen, (so be it).

_____

_____

Day Thirty-four

Psalm 18:1-6, 16,

_____ loves the Lord fervently and devotedly, O Lord, his/her strength. The Lord is _____'s Rock, his/her Fortress, and his/her Deliverer; his/her God, his/her keen and firm Strength in whom _____ will trust and take refuge, his/her Shield, and the Horn of his/her salvation, his/her High Tower. _____ will call upon the Lord, Who is to be praised; so shall _____ be saved from his/her enemies. The cords or bands of death surrounded _____, and the streams of ungodliness and the torrents of ruin terrified him/her. The cords of Sheol (the place of the dead) surrounded him/her; the snares of death confronted and came upon him/her. In his/her distress [when seemingly closed in] _____ called upon the Lord and cried to God: He heard his/her voice out of His temple (heavenly dwelling place), and his/her cry came before Him, into His [very] ears. He reached from on high, He took _____; He drew him/her out of many waters.

Miracles are coming! Keep praying...

_____
_____
_____
_____
_____
_____
_____
_____
_____
_____
_____
_____
_____
_____
_____

Day Thirty-five
Psalm 18:17, 28, 29, 30, 33, 34, 35

He delivered _____ from his/her strong enemy and from those who hated and abhorred _____, for they were too strong for him/her. For You cause _____'s lamp to be lighted and to shine; the Lord our God illumines his/her darkness. For by You, Lord _____ can run through a troop, and by our God _____ can leap over a wall. As for God, His way is perfect! The word of the Lord is tested and tried; He is a shield to _____ who takes refuge and puts his/her trust in Him. He makes _____'s feet like hinds' feet [able to stand firmly or make progress on the dangerous heights of testing and trouble]; He sets _____ securely upon his/her high places. He teaches _____'s hands to war, so that his/her arms can bend a bow of bronze.

God has given _____ the shield of His salvation, and the Father God's right hand has held _____ up; God's gentleness and condescension have made _____ great in Jesus' name. Amen, (so be it).

_____

_____

_____

_____

_____

_____

_____

_____

_____

_____

_____

_____

_____

_____

_____

_____

_____

Day Thirty-six
Psalm 18:36-45

You, Father God, have given plenty of room for _____'s steps under him/her, that his/her feet would not slip. _____ pursued his/her enemies and overtook them; neither did _____ turn again till they were consumed. _____ smote them so that they were not able to rise; they fell wounded under his/her feet. For You, Lord, have girded _____ with strength for the battle; You have subdued under him/her and caused to bow down those who rose up against him/her. You, Lord, have also made _____'s enemies turn their backs to him/her, that he/she might cut off those who hate him/her. They cried [for help], but there was none to deliver even unto the Lord, but You, Lord, answered them not. Then _____ beat them small as the

dust before the wind; _____
emptied them out as the dirt and mire
of the streets. You, Lord, have delivered
_____ from the strivings of the
people; You made him/her the head of
nations;   a people he/she had not
known served him/her. As soon as they
heard of _____, they obeyed
him/her; foreigners submitted themselves cringingly and yielded feigned
obedience to him/her. Foreigners lost
heart and came trembling out of their
caves or strongholds.

(This could be demonic strongholds and places of hiding! Foreigners
are those who are not in the family or
under the family covering. For example: demons are foreigners to God.
They are not like God. They are differ-
ent, foreign to Him, so think on that as
you pray this prayer)!

Day Thirty-
seven
Psalm 18:46-50

The Lord lives! Blessed be _____'s Rock; and let the God of _____'s salvation be exalted. The God Who avenges _____ and subdues peoples under him/her, Who delivers _____ from his/her enemies; yes, You, Lord, lift _____ up above those who rise up against him/her; You deliver him/her from the man of violence. Therefore will _____ give thanks and exalt You, Lord, among the nations, and sing praises to Your Name. Great deliverances and triumphs gives He to His king; and He shows mercy and steadfast love to his anointed, and to his/her offspring forever, in the mighty name of Jesus. Amen (so be it)!

(Remember, when praying this type of warfare prayer that the enemy can be a natural man or a supernatural demonic

force that has been sent against God's people. Don't concern yourself with the
enemy. God will take care of you. Focus
on God when you pray!)

_____

_____

_____

_____

_____

_____

_____

_____

Day Thirty-
eight

Matthew 10:31-32

_____ will not fear, for _____ is (are) of more value than many sparrows to the Lord. Therefore, _____ acknowledges Jesus before men and confesses Jesus [out of a state of oneness with Jesus]. Jesus will also acknowledge _____ before the Father God Who is in heaven and _____ will confess [that Jesus is abiding in] him/her, in Jesus' name. Amen, (so be it).

_____

_____

_____

_____

_____

_____

_____

_____

I thank You, Lord, that You give to _____ the keys of the kingdom of heaven; and whatever _____ binds (declares to be improper and unlawful) on earth must be what is already bound in heaven; and whatever _____ looses (declares lawful) on earth must be what is already loosed in heaven in Jesus' mighty name. Amen, (so be it).

Binding and loosing is very important to God — so do it!

_____

_____

_____

_____

_____

_____

_____

Day Forty
Matthew 18:18-20

I thank You, Lord, that whatever _____ forbid(s) and declare(s) to be improper and unlawful on earth must be what is already forbidden in heaven, and whatever _____ permit(s) and declares proper and lawful on earth must be what is already permitted in heaven. I thank You, Lord, that when _____ and anyone else on the earth agree (harmonize together, making a symphony together) about whatever [anything and everything] that they may ask, it will come to pass and be done for them by My Father in heaven. I thank You, Lord, that wherever two or three are gathered together in Your name, there You are in the midst of them.

(Remember, the above scriptures tell us that God has given to us two keys to the Kingdom of heaven. They are: #1 binding, #2 loosing.)

Where our prayers are concerned I like to end these past two days of praying with the following:

I thank You, Lord, that I declare the following to be improper and unlawful on earth concerning my family, friends, staff and ministry partners: poverty, sickness, disease, plague, dishonest, speech, fleshly talk, unrighteousness, doubt, unbelief, demonic captivity, suicide, anorexia, bulimia, overeating, depression, oppression, rebellion, any attack from demonic forces of any kind, turmoil, strife, ungodly thoughts and actions, abuse, (and any others you may think of). All these are already unlawful and improper in heaven, therefore, we have a right and we take our rightful authority to declare all of these things listed to be bound, inoperative, and ineffective in all of the people named before. These things are not permitted. They are not lawful on this earth concerning our family, friends, staff, and ministry family.

I thank You, Lord, that I declare to be proper and lawful on this earth in our family, friends, staff, and ministry family, by our rightful God given authority these following things. Prosperity is proper and lawful. It is loosed over us. Health, healing, freedom, peace, tranquility, protection from all human, inhuman, and demonic enemies, submissiveness, obedience, faith, hope, love, godly speech, godly mouths and tongues, godly thoughts and actions are all loosed over us. These are all activated, effective, operational, and loosed in our lives today in Jesus' name. Amen, (so be it).

Now remember to pray in your prayer language, the Holy Spirit of God, each day.

A place for your prayer thoughts.

_____

_____

_____

_____

_____

_____

_____

_____

_____

_____

_____

_____

_____

_____

_____

_____

_____

_____

_____

_____

_____

_____

_____

_____

Since you have finished praying all 40 days, now start over tomorrow and pray these 40 days of scripture prayers again! Add to your prayer list as you feel led of the Holy Spirit to do so. As you discipline yourself to spend this time each day in prayer for yourself and others I know that you will begin to see, feel, and know a change in yourself and in others. You are filling yourself with God's Word and you are also putting it into the atmosphere by speaking it to the Father God in prayer. He really does watch over His Word to perform it and you are allowing that to happen by your obedience to pray. This really makes the devil mad because he doesn't want you to take your God given rightful authority in the spirit realm...so do it again!!

The effectual fervent prayer of a righteous man (male and female) avails much so get with it! Let's get to availing much in our lives through   righteous prayer to our Heavenly Father God!

Pray, friends, pray! Remember, you may be the only one who will be obedient to pray for certain ones. Do it. Don't put it off or expect someone else to do it. It's your calling. Speak the Word of God out of your mouth and watch God perform His Word. He will do His part, never worry! It's rightfully ours, so take it!

If we don't partake of the work of Christ on the Cross, we are saying that what He did was in vain. No! What Christ did was not in vain! Receive today!

The Word works when you work the Word!

Order Form

Books	Price	Qty.
Being #1 at Being #2—Success Through Servanthood & Leadership	$10.00	_____
It's Too Soon to Give Up! Overcoming Depression as a Family	$ 8.00	_____
An Angels' Touch	$16.00	_____
For Men Only	$ 7.00	_____
Warriors of the Word (Includes Book #1 and #2 of children's comic book)	$ 5.00	_____
A Royal Child	$ 8.00	_____
Abuse...Bruised but not Broken —Breaking the Curse	$ 5.00	_____
The Mommy Book	$10.00	_____

Video/Audio Teaching Tapes

	Price	Qty.
Harvest Time for Your Family (5 audios/4 videos)	$20.00/$40.00	_____
Wahoo/Yahoo! (1 audio/1 video)	$5.00/$15.00	_____

Poster

	Price	Qty.
Protected (Michael, Natzar, Shalom)	$ 5.00	_____

Music

	Price	Qty.
Healing In This House (cassette)	$10.00	_____
From Our Children To You Harry III, Roman, Gabrielle (cassette)	$10.00	_____

For booking or to order additional titles of books, tapes or CD's, please contact us at:

Salem Family Ministries
P.O. Box 701287 • Tulsa, OK 74170
918-298-0770 FAX: 918-298-2517

Harry and Cheryl Salem

Harry Salem II grew up in Flint, Michigan. After his father's death in 1968, he relocated with his family to Florida. In 1980, he joined Oral Roberts Ministries, and at the age of twenty-six became vice-president of operations, crusade director and director of television production. In his work as author, television writer, producer and director he has won several Angel and Addy Awards. His most recent achievement was writing the successful book, *For Men Only*.

Cheryl Salem grew up in Choctaw County, Mississippi, and overcame many challenges on her journey to becoming Miss America in 1980. She is an accomplished author, speaker, musician, recording artist and teacher. She has recorded ten albums and CDs and has written numerous books, including her autobiography, *A Bright Shining*

Place, and her most recent, *The Mommy Book.* She continues to cohost the popular national daily program, *Make Your Day Count.*

Together Harry and Cheryl form Salem Family Ministries, which focuses on family. They stress the unity of family, marriage, personal relationships, financial goals and parenting as well as leading motivational meetings on overcoming obstacles, such as abuse, abandonment, poor self-image and financial problems. They have written over sixteen books together, including *An Angel's Touch, It's Too Soon to Give Up* and their most recent release, *Being #1 at Being #2.*

When not in their home in Tulsa, Oklahoma, the Salems continue to minister full-time throughout the world with their three children, Harry III, Roman and Gabrielle.

Additional copies of this book are
available from your local bookstore.

HARRISON HOUSE
Tulsa, Oklahoma 74153

The Harrison House Vision

Proclaiming the truth and the power
Of the Gospel of Jesus Christ
With excellence;

Challenging Christians to
Live Victoriously,
Grow Spiritually,
Know God intimately.